Boxes for Max

The Sound of X

By Marv Alinas

This is Max.

Max is six.

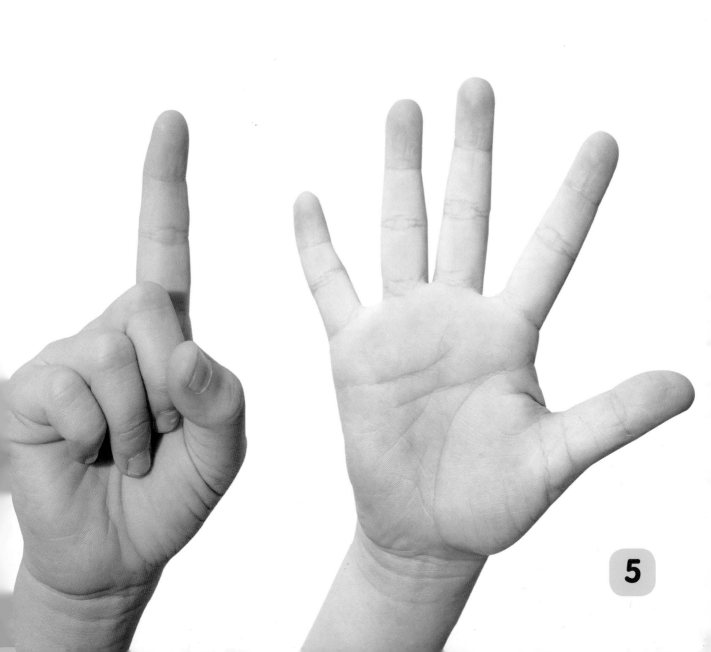

5

Max likes to fix boxes.

The boxes are not the same.

9

10

One box has a tux.

One box has
a toy ax.

13

One box has a toy fox.

One box has six cupcakes.

17

One box has
six eggs.

The last box has a toy *T-rex*!

21

Word List:

ax	Max
box	six
boxes	*T-rex*
fix	tux
fox	

Note to Parents and Educators

The books in this series are based on current research, which supports the idea that our brains are pattern-detectors rather than rules-appliers. This means children learn to read easier when they are taught the familiar spelling patterns found in English. As children encounter more complex words, they have greater success in figuring out these words by using the spelling patterns.

Throughout the series, the texts provide the reader with the opportunity to practice and apply knowledge of the sounds in natural language. The books introduce sounds using familiar onsets and *rimes*, or spelling patterns, for reinforcement.

For example, the word *cat* might be used to present the short "a" sound, with the letter *c* being the onset and "_at" being the rime. This approach provides practice and reinforcement of the short "a" sound, as there are many familiar words made with the "_at" rime.

The stories and accompanying photographs in this series are based on time-honored concepts in children's literature: well-written, engaging texts and colorful, high-quality photographs combine to produce books that children want to read again and again.

Dr. Peg Ballard
Minnesota State University, Mankato

The Child's World®
childsworld.com

Published by The Child's World®
1980 Lookout Drive • Mankato, MN 56003-1705
800-599-READ • www.childsworld.com

ACKNOWLEDGMENTS
The Child's World®: Mary Swensen, Publishing Director
The Design Lab: Design
Michael Miller: Editing

PHOTO CREDITS
© Africa Studio/Shutterstock.com: 18; Chanclos/
Shutterstock.com: 17; enchanted_fairy/Shutterstock.com:
14; Happy Together/Shutterstock.com: 5; LuckyImages/
Shutterstock.com: cover, 2, 6; metha1819/Shutterstock.
com: 21; posteriori/Shutterstock.com: 10; Venus
Angel/Shutterstock.com: 13; www.BillionPhotos.com/
Shutterstock.com: 9

ISBN 9781503809253
LCCN 2015958491

Printed in the United States of America
Mankato, MN
June, 2016
PA02310

ABOUT THE AUTHOR

Marv Alinas has worked in children's
educational publishing for 20 years. When
she is not reading or writing, Marv enjoys
spending time with her husband and dogs
and traveling to interesting places. Marv
lives in Minnesota.